I Know Why Birds Fight For A
Position On The Power-Line

I Know Why Birds Fight For A Position On The Power-Line

—ww—

Fight For Your Position On The Power-Line

Volume 1

Kathy Buckner

I Know Why Birds Fight For A Position On The Power-Line
Stay Connected To The Power-Line
All Rights Reserved
Copyright © 2017 Kathy Buckner
v1.0

This book may not be reproduced, transmitted, or stored in whole or in part by any means, including graphic, electronic, or mechanical without the express written consent of the publisher except in the case of brief quotations embodied in critical articles and reviews.
ISBN-13: 9780998780917
ISBN-10: 099878091X
Scripture quotations marked AMP are taken from The Amplified® Bible. Copyright 1954, 1958, 1962, 1964, 1965, 1987, 2015 by The Lockman Foundation. Used by permission. Scripture quotations marked NASB are taken from the New American Standard Bible. Copyright 1960, 1962, 1963, 1968, 1971, 1972, 1973, 1975, 1977, 1995 by The Lockman Foundation. Used by permission. Scripture quotations marked AMPC are taken from the Amplified Bible Classic Edition, Copyright 1954, 1958, 1962, 1946, 1965, 1987, by The Lockman Foundation. Used by permission. Scripture quotations marked BBE are taken from The Bible in Basic English. Scriptures marked in CEB are taken from the Common English Bible. Copyright by Common English Bible Committee and the Christian Resource Development Corporation Inc., Nashville, Tennessee. All rights reserved. Used by permission. Scripture quotations marked NIV are taken from the Holy Bible, New International Version, Copyright 1973, 1978, 1984, 2010 International Bible Society. Used by permission of Zondervan. All right reserved. Scripture quotations marked NKJV are taken from the New King James Version. Copyright 1982 by Thomas Nelson, Inc. Used by permission. All rights reserved. Scripture quotations marked KJV are taken from the King James Version. All rights reserved. Scripture quotations marked CEV are taken from the Contemporary English Version. Copyright by the American Bible Society, New York, N.Y. All rights reserved. Scripture quotations marked NLT are taken from the Holy Bible, New Living Translation. Copyright 1996, 2004 Used by permission of Tyndale House Publishers, Wheaton, Illinois 60189. All rights reserved. Scripture quotations marked NET are taken from the New English Translation Bible. Copyright 1996-2016 by Biblical Studies Press L.L.C. All rights reserved. Used with permission. Scripture quotations of ESV are taken from the Holy Bible English Standard Version (ESV). Copyright 2001 Crossway, a publishing ministry of Good News Publishers. Used by permission. Scripture quotations marked MSG are taken from The Message Version. Copyright 1994, 1995, 1996, 2000, 2001, 2002. Used by permission of NavPress Publishing Group. Scripture quotations marked by WEB are taken from the World Wide English Bible. Public Domain.
Scripture quotations marked LEB are taken from the Lexham English Bible. Copyright 2010 Logo Bible Software. Used by permission. Scripture quotations marked GNB are taken the Good News Bible (GNB). Copyright 1994 published by the Bible Societies/HarperCollins Publisher Ltd., Good News Bible American Bible Society 1966, 1971, 1976, 1992. Used by permission. Scripture quotations marked NLT are taken from the Holy Bible, New Living Translation, copyright 1996, 2004, 2007 Tyndale House Foundation. Used by permission of Tyndale House Publishers, Inc., Carol Stream, Illinois 60188. All rights reserved. Scripture quotations marked GW are taken from God's Word, copyright 1995 by God's Word to the Nations. All rights reserved. Used with permission. Scriptures marked NCV are taken from the New Century Version. Copyright 2005 by Thomas Nelson, Inc. All rights reserved. Used by permission.
Scripture quotations marked GNT are taken from the Good News Translation (U.S. Version, Second Edition) © 1992 American Bible Society. All rights reserved. Used by permission. Scripture quotations marked GNB are taken the Good News Bible (GNB). Copyright 1994 published by the Bible Societies/HarperCollins Publisher Ltd., Good News Bible American Bible Society 1966, 1971, 1976, 1992. Used with Permission. Good News Bible (Anglecised) Published by the British and foreign Bible Society. Copyright 1992.
Scripture quotation marked GNB are taken from the Good News Bible with Deuterocanonicals/Apocrypha. Copyright 1992 British and foreign Bible Society. Used with permission. Scripture quotations marked DARBY are taken from Darby English Bible. Public domain. Scripture quotation marked ASV are taken from American Standard Version. Public domain. Scripture quotations marked NHEB are taken from New Heart English Bible. Public domain. Scripture quotations marked NIRV are taken from the New International Reader's Version, NIRV Copyright 1995, 1996, 1998, 2014 by Biblica, Inc. Used by permission of Zondervan. All rights reserved.
All rights reserved - used with permission PRINTED IN THE UNITED STATES OF AMERICA.
PRIMARY EDITOR WAS JANELLA BUCKNER.
COVER DESIGN BY ALEJANDRO ARRIBAS, ALTAGRAPHICS

Contents

Foreword · vii

Believe · 1
Faith · 9
Confusion · 15
Let it Go · 21
I Stand Tall · 25
Now, Faith Is · 31
Holy Spirit · 39
My Faults are in a Vault · 45
A Prayer for a Teenager · · · · · · · · · · · · · · · · · · · 53
The Lion's Den · 61
Old Fashioned Common Sense · · · · · · · · · · · · · 65
The Day I Cried for a Friend · · · · · · · · · · · · · · · 71
Get Up Now · 77
Spirit of God · 83
You are not Alone · 89
The Day I Threw a Kiss to the World · · · · · · · · · 95

Foreword

Devote yourselves to prayer, being watchful and thankful (Colossian 4:2 NIV).

Gratitude

God will *always* love you forever. Daily praise is due because of His unfailing love. Start by giving thanks for His peace, joy, love, kindness, and gentleness.

Give thanks to the Lord, for he is good; his love endures forever (Psalms107:1 NIV). *"Let them give thanks to the Lord for his unfailing love and his wonderful deeds for mankind..."* (Psalms 107:8, 15, 21, 31 NIV). This is stated four times in this chapter. Praise is due for God's wonderful work. You get the benefits for showing gratitude.

Let them sacrifice thank offerings and tell of His works with songs of joy (Psalms107:22 NIV). God shows His love for you every day. Look in the sky every morning. He set boundaries for the waters. He has total control of everything that's in the deep waters. He deserves all praise for the past, present, and the future. *Let the one who is wise heed these things and ponder the loving deeds of the Lord* (Psalms 107:43 NIV).

When God's people mature, others will understand the love of God as they see joy and happiness flowing.

For all things are for your sakes, so that the grace which is spreading to more and more people may cause the giving of thanks to abound to the glory of God (2 Corinthians 4:15 KJV).

You can never give enough thanks for all that God has done. When you give thanks, you become selfless. Desire for material things will not be as great because you begin to have a clearer perspective of what is temporal and eternal.

Footsteps

Every step that you take is important for progress. You will experience great peace when you stay connected to God's powerline and follow His lead. *God is able to bless you abundantly, so that in all things at all times, having all that you need, you will abound in every good work* (2Corinthian 9:8 NIV).

Jesus Christ is the vine and His followers are the branches. These are the instructions that He presented to you. Think of it as you would if everything that exists connected to the internet.

I am the vine; you are the branches. If you remain in me and I in you, you will bear much fruit; apart from me you can do nothing. If you do not remain in me, you are like a branch that is thrown away and withers; such branches are picked up, thrown into the fire and burned. If you remain in me and my words remain in you, ask whatever you wish, and it will be done for you. This is to my Father's glory, that you bear much fruit, showing yourselves to be my disciples. As the Father has loved me, so have I loved you. Now remain in my love (John 15, 5-9 NIV).

Promises and Power

Brothers, let me put this in human terms. Even a human covenant, once it is ratified, cannot be canceled or amended (Galatians 3:5 NIV).

For if the inheritance depends on the Law, then it no longer depends on a promise; but God freely granted it to Abraham through a promised (Galatians 3:18 NIV). God can not lie. Waiting is hard and it can be long. Hope and trust in God are mandatory. You should plead our case with God's promises.

And if we are children, then we are heirs: heirs of God and co-heirs with Christ--if indeed we suffer with Him, so that we may also be glorified with Him (Romans 8:17 NIV). *And if you belong to Christ, then you are Abraham's seed and heirs according to the promise* (Galatians 3:29 NIV).

I Have Spoken!!

It is written: But having the same spirit of faith, according to what is written, "I BELIEVED, THEREFORE, I SPOKE" we also believe, therefore we also speak, knowing that He who raised the Lord Jesus will raise us also with Jesus and will present us with you (2 Corinthians 4:13 NSAB).

Truly I tell you, if anyone says to this mountain, 'Go, throw yourself into the sea,' and does not doubt in their heart but believes that what they say will happen, it will be done for them (Matthew 11:23 NIV). *He replied, "Because you have so little faith. Truly I tell you, if you have faith as small as a mustard seed, you can say to this mountain, 'Move from here to there,' and it will move. Nothing will be impossible for you* (Matthew. 17:20 NIV).

If I have the gift of prophecy and can fathom all mysteries and all knowledge, and if I have a faith that can move mountains, but do not have love, I am nothing (1 Corinthians 13:2 NIV).

Let love and faithfulness never leave you; bind them around your neck, write them on the tablet of your heart (Proverb 3:3 NIV).

Be alert and of sober mind. Your enemy the devil prowls around like a roaring lion looking for someone to devour (1 Peter 5:8 NIV). *When God made his promise to Abraham, since there was no one greater for him to swear by, he swore by himself, saying "I will surely bless you and give you many descendant"* (Hebrew 6:13 NIV).

You need to take charge of the purpose that God has placed in you.

You will also declare a thing and it will be established for you; so, your light will shine on your ways (Job 22:28 NIV).

Believe

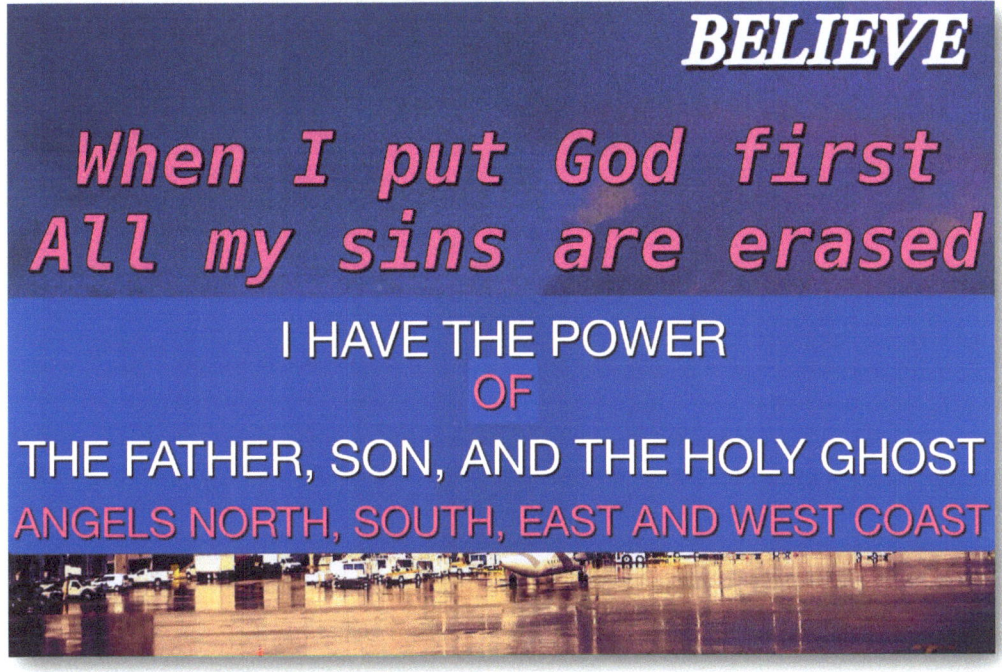

BELIEVE

For the Father leads me,
The Holy Spirit
Gives me comfort
And for me, the Son intercedes
I have love

Unconditionally and eternally
Favor and freedom generously

—MESSAGE ALERT— **BELIEVE**

I have the mind of Christ—
God sent His Son because I need to have
The Holy Spirit inside of my body,
When I want to live large,
Feel enticed

To be proud, hateful, and cruel
He reminds me that He's in charge
For He gives food so that I can enjoy a feast

His love for me
Gives me joy, strength, and remarkable peace

BELIEVE

I now put Him first,
Because I am no longer under the curse
He gives me a clean heart and
Never remembers my past
Every sunrise, I get new mercies
Instantaneously, I receive
Truth and grace endlessly
I have the keys to the kingdom of heaven
Because He wants me to love completely
And eternally
He loves me so much that He had His child
To come into this world to be humiliated

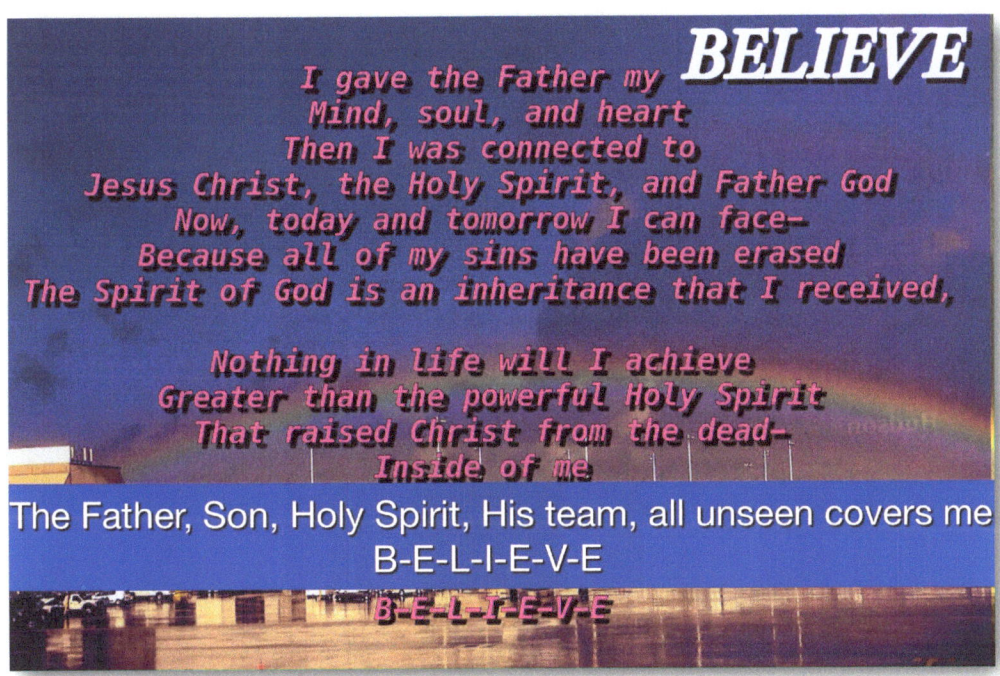

Gratitude

I thank the Lord for faith.
Victories that were won at the cross on my behalf make me completely thankful.
I thank the Lord for teaching me how to walk by faith.
I thank God for helping me understand why I need to always put Him first.

Footsteps

Put God first.
Go in the strength of the Lord.
Believe and allow the power of God to instruct you. Know that God will work through you. Listen and expect God to give you instructions. Keep your heart physically fit and spiritually fit, for out of the heart are the issues of life. When God's word speaks to you, be obedient. The more you do what He ask of you, the more your faith will increase.

Prayer

Precious Father,
You are great and powerful. You have glory, victory, and honor. Everything in heaven and earth belongs to You. The kingdom belongs to You, Lord. You are ruler of everything. You have the power and strength to make anyone great and strong. I know that I have the favor of God and man. I bind every satanic force that comes against what God has planned my family and me. I release the power of God over my life. I surrender all to God; my body, my will, my mind, and my destination. I am joint heirs with Jesus Christ. Jesus came that I might have life and have it more abundantly. I receive my abundant life right now. I thank You for giving me the mind and the wisdom of Christ.

Promises and Power

"...but those who trust in the Lord will prosper" (Proverb 28:25 NIV).
Take delight in the Lord (the word), and He will give you the desires of your heart (Psalms 37:4 NIV).
Blessed is the Man who perseveres under trial because, having stood the test, that person will receive the crown of life that the Lord has promised those that love him (James1:12 NIV).

Without faith, it is impossible to please Him: for He that cometh to God must believe that He is, and that He is a rewarder of them that diligently seek Him. (Hebrews 11:6 KJV).
The young lions lack and suffer hunger; But those who seek the Lord shall not lack any good thing. (Psalm 34:10 NKJV).

I Have Spoken!!

I will have a relationship with God daily. I will diligently listen to God.
I will seek Him first.
I will allow myself to be used by Him.
I will go in the strength of the Lord and will not compromise my values.
I will speak His promises over my household.
I praise God for believing in me. He thought about me before He create the world.

Faith

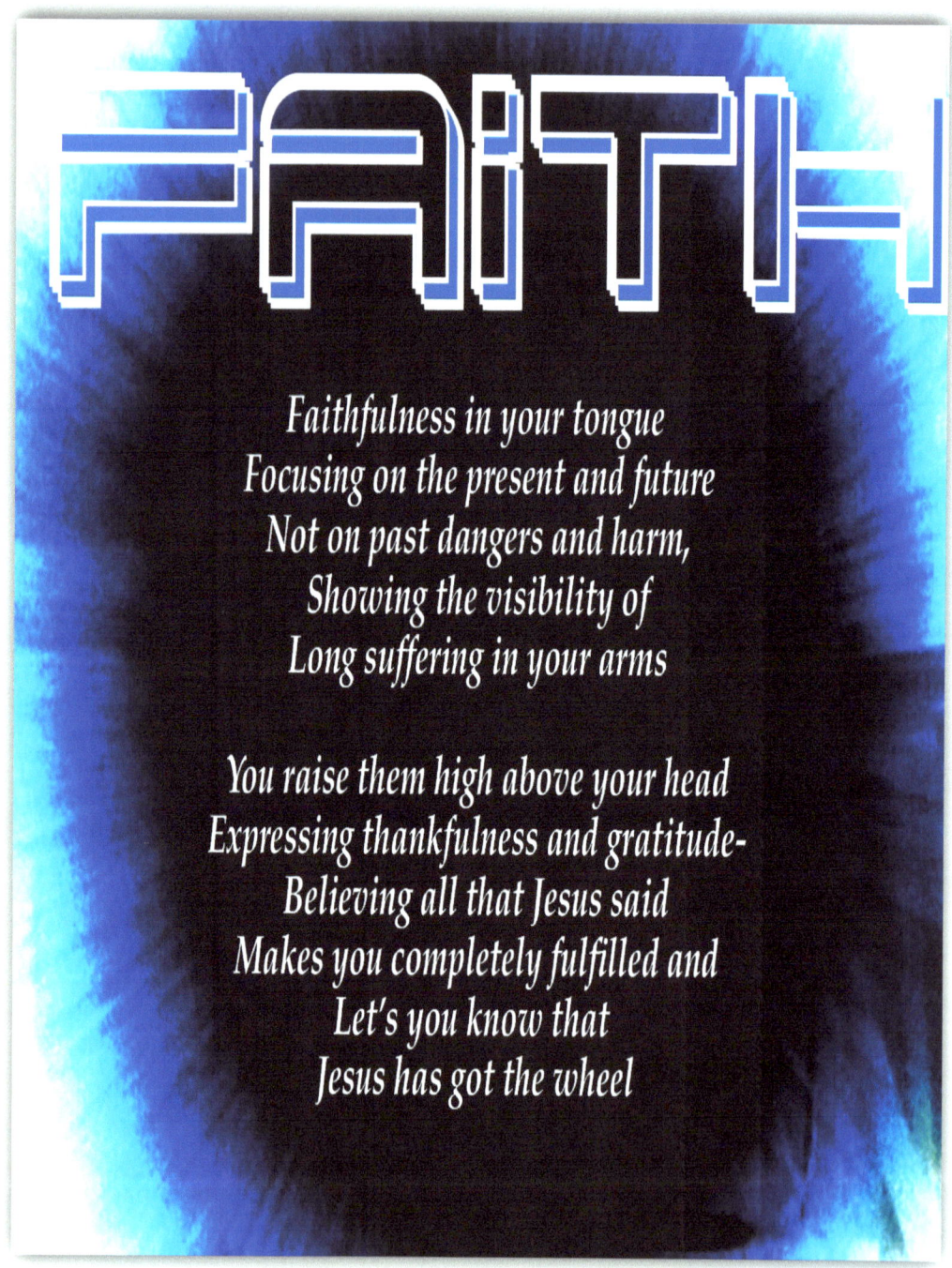

FAITH

Faithfulness in your tongue
Focusing on the present and future
Not on past dangers and harm,
Showing the visibility of
Long suffering in your arms

You raise them high above your head
Expressing thankfulness and gratitude-
Believing all that Jesus said
Makes you completely fulfilled and
Let's you know that
Jesus has got the wheel

Gratitude

Precious Father, I thank You
For never leaving me.
For guiding me and instructing me while I'm awake or sleeping.
For being my inheritance and my blessings.
For guarding all that is mine.
For the joy of your presence.
For having the opportunity to live with you forever.
(Psalms 16:5-11 NLT).

Footsteps

Read the scriptures.
Proclaim and declare the word.
Pray in the Spirit.
Do not worry. Seek God's face. Listen. Pray.
Speak to the mountain.
Ask for what you want.
Believe (have faith).
Receive it. You don't have to see it.
You must live in the unseen world as well as the seen world.
(Just because you don't see it doesn't mean that it does not exist.)

Start doing something where you can see faith at work.

- Say something kind to everyone.
- Give to someone before they ask.
- Don't rush to judge someone.
- Show someone love that you feel do not deserve it.
- Believe. God is His word. Take one step at a time.

Prayer

Precious Father,
I surrender all to You. Help me to be strong enough to leave everything behind me that does not line up with the word. I put all my trust in You. I worship only You. I seek humility today and cast down pride. I am grateful and thankful for all You do. I seek love, kindness, gentleness, self-control, compassion and increased faith. I refuse to be bitter, cruel, thoughtless and disrespectful. Father help me to love that person who is full of resentment and help me to do something nice for someone who is totally disrespectful.

Promises and Power

Peter remembered what Jesus had said to the tree on the previous day and exclaimed, "Look, Rabbi! The fig tree you cursed has withered and died!" Then Jesus said to the disciples, "Have faith in God. I tell you the truth, you can say to this mountain, 'May you be lifted up and thrown into the sea,' and it will happen. But you must really believe it will happen and have no doubt in your heart. I tell you, you can pray for anything, and if you believe that you've received it, it will be yours. But when you are praying, first forgive anyone you are holding a grudge against, so that your Father in heaven will forgive your sins, too " (Mark 11:21-25 NLT).
God's word is His faith.

To have faith is to be sure of the things we hope for, to be certain of the things we cannot see.
It is by faith that we understand that the universe was created by God's word, so that what can be seen was made of what cannot be seen (Hebrews 11:1, 3 GNTD).

Do you see what this means—all these pioneers who blazed the way, all these veterans cheering us on? It means we'd better get on with it. Strip down, start running, and never quit! No extra spiritual fat, no parasitic sins. Keep your eyes on Jesus, who both began and finished this race we're in. Study how Jesus did it. Because He never lost sight of where He was headed—that exhilarating finish in and with God—He could put up with anything along the way: cross, shame, whatever. And now He's there, in the place of honor, right alongside God. When you find yourselves flagging in your faith, go over that story again, item by item, that long litany of hostility Jesus plowed through. That will shoot adrenaline into your souls (Hebrews 12:1-3 MSG).

I Have Spoken!

I will walk in the unseen and the seen world.
I speak to those things that are not as if they were in front of me.
I deny myself today and totally lean on Jesus.
I will run this race forward and focusing on Jesus.

*The righteous keep moving forward, and those with clean hands become stronger and stronge*r (Job 17:9 NLT).
I praise God for His truth and faithfulness.

Confusion

Confusion,
This is not your place
You cannot build rooms with concrete
And lace it with crown molding
You brighten your space to be discrete
Peace is not allowed to lounge around
Regardless of the size of the building
This day confusion must go
For peace will remain still and sound
Only peace will come through those doors
Confusion you are bound
Forward, peace will flow–

Gratitude

Father,
I thank You for your wisdom, knowledge, and understanding that only You can give.
Thank You for your peace.
Thank You for allowing me to speak to the mountains of confusion to bring peace forward.

Footsteps

Walk out of your door with the attitude that you will be the person who will console others.
Encourage others.
Listen intently.
Enjoy and learn to appreciate the good around you.
Try not to comment about every statement you hear.
Listen and act on good advice.
Do not get agitated when someone offers advice.
Wait a few days before you decide to correct someone. You will find the best way to say what's needed in the most effective way.

Prayer

Precious Father,
Today, in my heart, soul, and mind
I release a benevolent loving spirit.
I leave behind this cruel, spiteful spirit.

I release an honest sincere spirit.
I leave behind this cold, deceitful spirit.

I release a respectful, gracious spirit.
I leave behind this slandering and bullying spirit.

I release a kind heartfelt spirit.
I leave behind this resentful, jealous spirit.

I will keep away from foolish and ignorant arguments; for I know that they end up in quarrels (2 Timothy 2:22, 23 GNT).

I ask my precious Father to help me control my hormones and greed.
I believe with God all things are possible.
I will strive to live right, increase my faith, love and be peaceful.
Avoid the passions of youth, and STRIVE for righteousness, faith, love, and peace, together with those who with a pure heart call out to the Lord for help. But keep away from foolish and ignorant arguments; you know that they end up in quarrels (2 Timothy 2:22, 23 GNT).
I will work with others to achieve success in mastering these desires.

Promises and Power

Commit your works to the LORD and your plans will be established (Romans 12:1 NASB).
Young (men and women) likewise exhort to be sober minded. In all things shewing thyself a pattern of good works: in doctrine shewing incorruptness, gravity, (seriousness) sincerity, Sound speech, that cannot be condemned; he that is of the contrary part maybe ashamed, having no evil thing to say of you (Titus 2:6-8 KJV). *So here's what I want you to do, God helping you: Take your everyday, ordinary life—your sleeping, eating, going-to-work, and walking-around life— and place it before God as an offering. Embracing what God does for you is the best thing you can do for Him. Don't become so well-adjusted to your culture that you fit into it without even thinking. Instead, fix your attention on God. You'll be changed from the inside out. Readily recognize what He wants from you, and quickly respond to it. Unlike the culture around you, always dragging you down to*

its level of immaturity, God brings the best out of you, develops well-formed maturity in you (Romans 12:1-2 MSG). *Therefore everyone who hears these words of mine and puts them into practice is like a wise man who built his house on the rock* (Matthew 7:24 NIV).

So get rid of all evil behavior. Be done with all deceit, hypocrisy, jealousy, and all unkind speech. Like newborn babies, you must crave pure spiritual milk so that you will grow into a full experience of salvation. Cry out for this nourishment, now that you have had a taste of the Lord's kindness (1 Peter 2:1-3, NLT).

I Have Spoken!

I will stay away from foolish and ignorant arguments.
I will strive to demonstrate faith, peace, and love.
I will strive to understand and be sensitive to the needs of others.
I will restrain from having a flippant tongue.
I will be a better listener.
I praise God for helping me control my tongue.

Let it Go

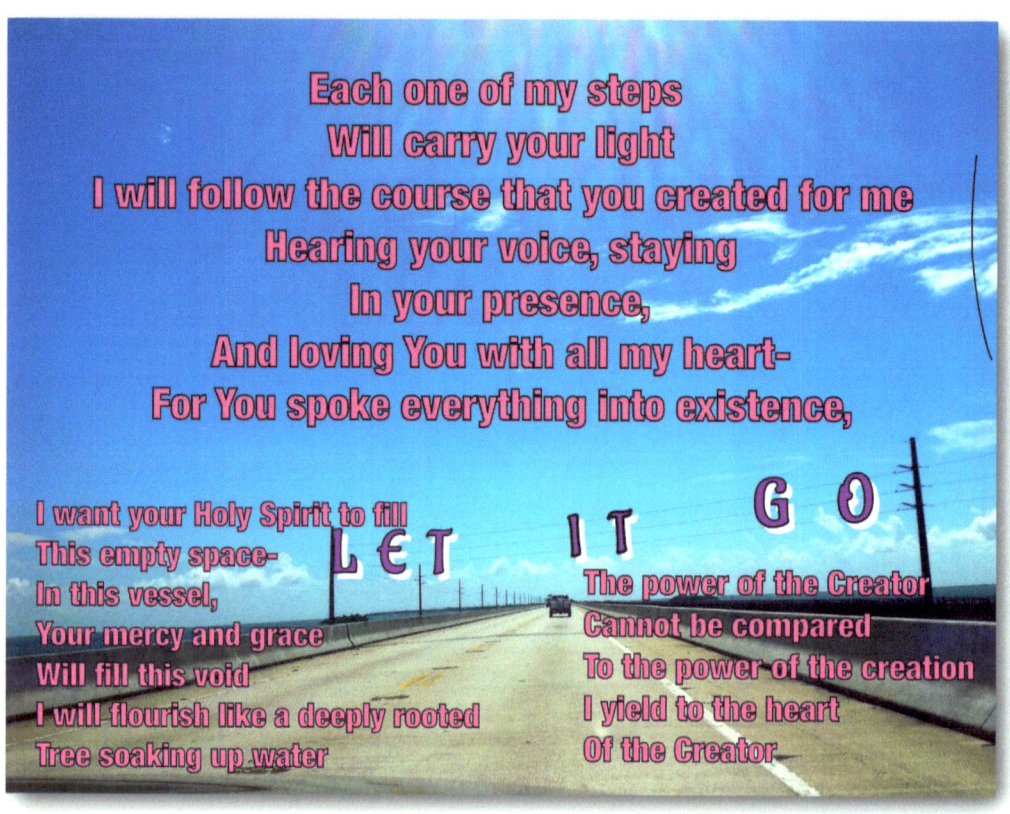

Gratitude

Precious Father,
Thank You being my Creator and giving me confidence to move forward in Your love.
Thank You for Your wisdom.
Thank You for teaching me how to let go of problems and difficult situations.

Footsteps

Trust God with all your heart.
Do not think that you are wiser than you are, for God gives wisdom.
Never rely on what you think you know.
Draw near to the Lord in everything that you do. He will show you what to do.
Give your best always and in all things.

Prayer

Precious Father,
Thank You for being my strength and support when I am weak. Help me let go of my past and move forward. Help me to always think on what is good, lovely, and things that make me smile. Help me enjoy each moment as I breathe with the breath that You've given me. Thank You Father for Your word which states, "*I will put my laws in their hearts, and I will write them on their minds.*" "*Their sins and lawless act I remember no more. And where these have been forgiven, sacrifice for sin is no longer necessary*" (Hebrews 10:16-18 NIVUK). God created everything in the unseen world as well as the seen world in six days. I will *not* focus on my past or bad things that can happen. Satan loves to meet me on that path. God does not remember my past. Hope is mandatory for faith.

I cannot please God without faith. Satan wants to keep my mind focused on all the troubles, past, bad things in the world, or things that could happen. I thank God for the patience school bus driver, the person who prays diligently in church, and each staff member who keeps the schools running smoothly.

Promises and Power

I do not mean that I am already as God wants me to be. I have not yet reached that goal, but I continue trying to reach it and to make it mine. Christ wants me to do that, which is the reason he made me his brothers and sisters. I know that I have not yet reached that goal, but there is one thing I always do. Forgetting the past and straining toward what is ahead, I keep trying to reach the goal and get the prize for which God called me through Christ to the life above (Philippians 3:12-14 NCV).
Therefore, do not worry about tomorrow for tomorrow will worry about itself. Each day has enough troubles of its own (Matthew 6:34 NIV).

"And do not be worried, for the joy of the LORD is your strength and your stronghold." (Nehemiah 8:10 AMP).

I—yes, I alone—will blot out your sins for my own sake and will never think of them again.
Let us review the situation together, and you can present your case to prove your innocence (Isaiah 43:25-26).

I Have Spoken!

I will humble myself in the presence of the Lord.
He will exalt me.
I will continually hope in the Lord.
I am living in the moment and refuse to go down the road of bitterness and resentment.
I praise God for giving my mind and spirit a makeover.

I Stand Tall

I Stand Tall

I stand tall
In this life
That I live
I'll keep
Inching forward
To gain a view
Of the goals
That I want
To achieve
I stand tall
I'll get another
Good break
The good will
Unfold
In this life
I will celebrate
As I learn from my mistakes
I stand tall
Every upward movement is
An advantage that
I'm gonna grab and take
This time
I stand tall
To reach an higher level
Beyond my tiptoes
Achieving a goal to
Stop wobbling from
Side to side

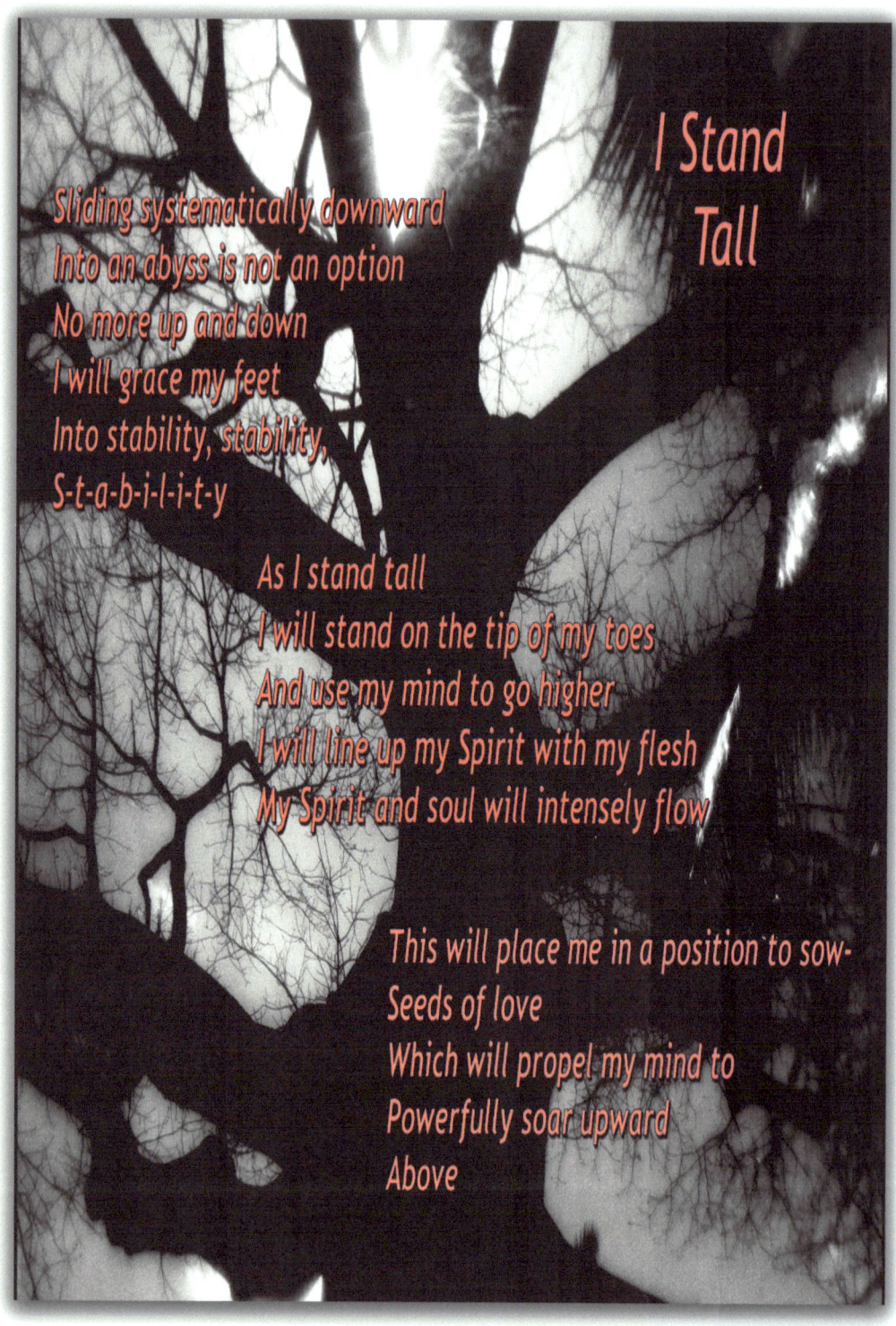

I Stand Tall

Sliding systematically downward
Into an abyss is not an option
No more up and down
I will grace my feet
Into stability, stability,
S-t-a-b-i-l-i-t-y

As I stand tall
I will stand on the tip of my toes
And use my mind to go higher
I will line up my Spirit with my flesh
My Spirit and soul will intensely flow

This will place me in a position to sow-
Seeds of love
Which will propel my mind to
Powerfully soar upward
Above

Gratitude

Father, thank You for daily shining Your goodness upon me and shielding me from all evil.

Anxiety in a man's heart weighs it down, but a good word makes it glad (Proverbs 12:25 NASB).

Pleasant words are a honeycomb, sweet to the soul and healing to the bones (Proverbs 16:24 NASB).

The spirit of a man can endure his sickness, but as for a broken spirit who can bear it? (Proverbs 18:14 NHEB)

Footsteps

Strive to put good thoughts in your mind when you wake up in the morning.
Put uplifting situations in your mind.
Start by removing all the bad thoughts out of your mind.
Speak to any bad thought that comes in your mind.
Uplifting thoughts and inspiring minds bring about invigorating times.
Start giving gratitude for the beauty in your environment.
Refuse any thoughts that are not in line with God's word and any thought that is not uplifting.
Sometimes you need to speak the Word to the thoughts in your mind.
Do not try to reason with those bad thoughts.
When you entertain those bad thoughts, they hang around a long time.
Make someone's day. Enjoy the people that you see as you go through your daily activities.
Really, let your light shine.

Prayer

Precious Father,
Help me enjoy you daily. Help me control the thoughts in my mind.

Search me, O God, and know my heart: try me, and know my thoughts: And see if there be any wicked way in me, and lead me in the way everlasting (Proverbs 139:23-24 KJV).
Help me to be joyful when others are blessed. Help me keep my thoughts on the word so that they will be pleasing to You.

Promises and Power

The Lord is our protector and glorious king, blessing us with kindness and honor. He does not refuse any good thing to those who do what is right. Lord Almighty, how happy are those who trust in you (Psalm 84:11 GNT)!

I will tell of the Lord's unfailing love; I praise him for all he has done for us. He has richly blessed the people of Israel because of his mercy and constant love (Isaiah 63:7 GNT).

Let this same attitude and purpose and [humble] mind be in you which was in Christ Jesus: [Let Him be your example in humility:] Who, although being essentially one with God and in the form of God [possessing the fullness of the a tributes which make God God], did not think this equality with God was a thing to be eagerly grasped or retained, But stripped Himself [of all privileges and righteously dignity], so as to assume the guise of a servant (slave), in that He became like men and was born a human being (Philippians 2:5-7 AMPC).

He forms all their thoughts and knows everything they do (PS 33:21 GNT).

Do not allow bad thoughts to dominate your mind and harden your heart.

The Lord hates the thoughts of sinful people. But the thoughts of pure people are pleasing to him (Proverbs 15:26 NIRV).

Lean not to your own understanding, trust in The Lord (Proverbs 3:5 NLT).

God began doing a good work in you, and I am sure he will continue it until it is finished when Jesus Christ comes again (Philippians 1:6 NCV).

I Have Spoken!

I will go forward in the mind and the attitude of the Lord.
I will not focus on what I think that I understand.
I am trusting in the Lord for all that I do.
I will walk in the Spirit and the wisdom of God.
I will stop every bad thought and vision that comes in my mind against God's word.
I praise God for helping me control my mind.

Say it aloud! I will cast down imaginations of every high thing that exalteth itself against the knowledge of God and take captive every thought to make it obedient to Christ. (2Corinthians 10:5).

Casting down imaginations, and every high thing that exalteth itself against the knowledge of God, and bringing into captivity every thought to the obedience of Christ; And having in a readiness to revenge all disobedience, when your obedience is fulfilled (2 Corinthians 10:5 KJV).

Learn this so that you can say it any time something is disturbing in your thoughts.
If He can put your past out of His mind; I know that He can put your past out of your mind.

Now, Faith Is

Gratitude

Father, thank You for allowing me to talk directly to You.
I thank You for winning all my battles for me.
The victory is won.
I'm grateful that You know the best solution to solve my problems, because You made me.

Footsteps

1. When you recognize a problem, speak life to the solution, speak to fear, (many problems are only in your mind), and stay true to your position.
2. Control your thoughts. Try not to blame, doubt, compare, or go back and forth with the solutions.
3. Answer the thoughts in your mind with the word of God. (It's sharper than the sharpest double-edged sword.) Speak aloud.
4. Indulge in God's love and read about the power of God.
5. Understand that the victory is yours to receive.
6. Be humble. (Don't worry about what people are saying.)
7. Get involved with helping others when your patience becomes short.
8. Sing or listen to some of your favorite songs.
9. Never stop trusting and believing God.
10. Speak what the Word says.
11. Some of your friends may not understand. You might have to step back from some relationships. This is hard some times.

Prayer

Precious Father
With Your words (promises) all things were made.
With Your words, all things are possible because You are Your word; as stated in Genesis: In the beginning was the word and the word was God. (Genesis 1:1 KJV) We have air and oxygen; however, no man can see it.
You can make the wind blow softly or with great power; no man can see it.
You can make the waves gust with great power or softly.
There is no other god as powerful as Jehovah.
Your son died on the cross and ascended so that we could have a Comforter.
No other god is more loving as Jehovah.
You raised men from the dead; no other god is as loving as Jehovah.
You make the blind see; no other god is as loving as Jehovah.
You make the lame walk; no other god is as loving as Jehovah.
You turn the hearts of kings; no other god is as loving as Jehovah.
You free the mind of the mentally disturbed; no other god is as loving as Jehovah.
Thank You for Your love, peace, grace, and Your word.

Promises and Power

God rescued us from dead-end alleys and dark dungeons. He's set us up in the kingdom of the Son he loves so much, the Son who got us out of the pit we were in, got rid of the sins we were doomed to keep repeating (Colossian 1:13-14 MSG).

What you say can preserve life or destroy it; so you must accept the consequences of your words (Proverbs 18:21 GNT).

Death gets its power to hurt from sin, and sin gets its power from the Law. But thanks be to God who gives us the victory through our Lord Jesus Christ (1Corinthians 15:57-58 GNT)!

Let love and faithfulness never leave you; bind them around your neck, write them on the tablet of your heart. Then you will win favor and a good name in the sight of God and man (Proverbs 3:3, 4 NIV). *Trust in the Lord with all your heart. Never rely on what you think you know. Remember the Lord in everything you do, and he will show you the right way. Never let yourself think that you are wiser than you are; simply obey the Lord and refuse to do wrong. If you do, it will be like good medicine, healing your wounds and easing your pains. Honor the Lord by making him an offering from the best of all that your land produces. If you do, your barns will be filled with grain, and you will have too much wine to store it all* (Proverbs 3:5-10 GNT).

Do your own work well, and then you will have something to be proud of. But don't compare yourself with others (Galatians 6:4 CEV).
I pray that the gifts that You have blessed me with will be used for your glory!

My child, if you become wise, I will be very happy.
I will be proud when I hear you speaking words of wisdom.
Don't be envious of sinful people; let reverence for the Lord be the concern of your life. If it is, you have a bright future.
Listen, my child, be wise and give serious thought to the way you live. Don't associate with people who drink too much wine or stuff themselves with food.
Drunkards and gluttons will be reduced to poverty. If all you do is eat and sleep, you will soon be wearing rags.

Listen to your father; without him you would not exist. When your mother is old, show her your appreciation.
A righteous person's parents have good reason to be happy. You can take pride in a wise child.
Let your father and mother be proud of you; give your mother that happiness (Proverbs 23: 15-25 GNT).

I Have Spoken!

Father, I declare that victory is mine.
Nothing will take my hope from me.
My focus is on the power of God.
I will follow the Holy Spirit and search for wisdom and knowledge to get the most out of my gifts and talents.
I give You all the glory for all my blessings and answered prayers.
I praise God for giving me words of wisdom.

Holy Spirit

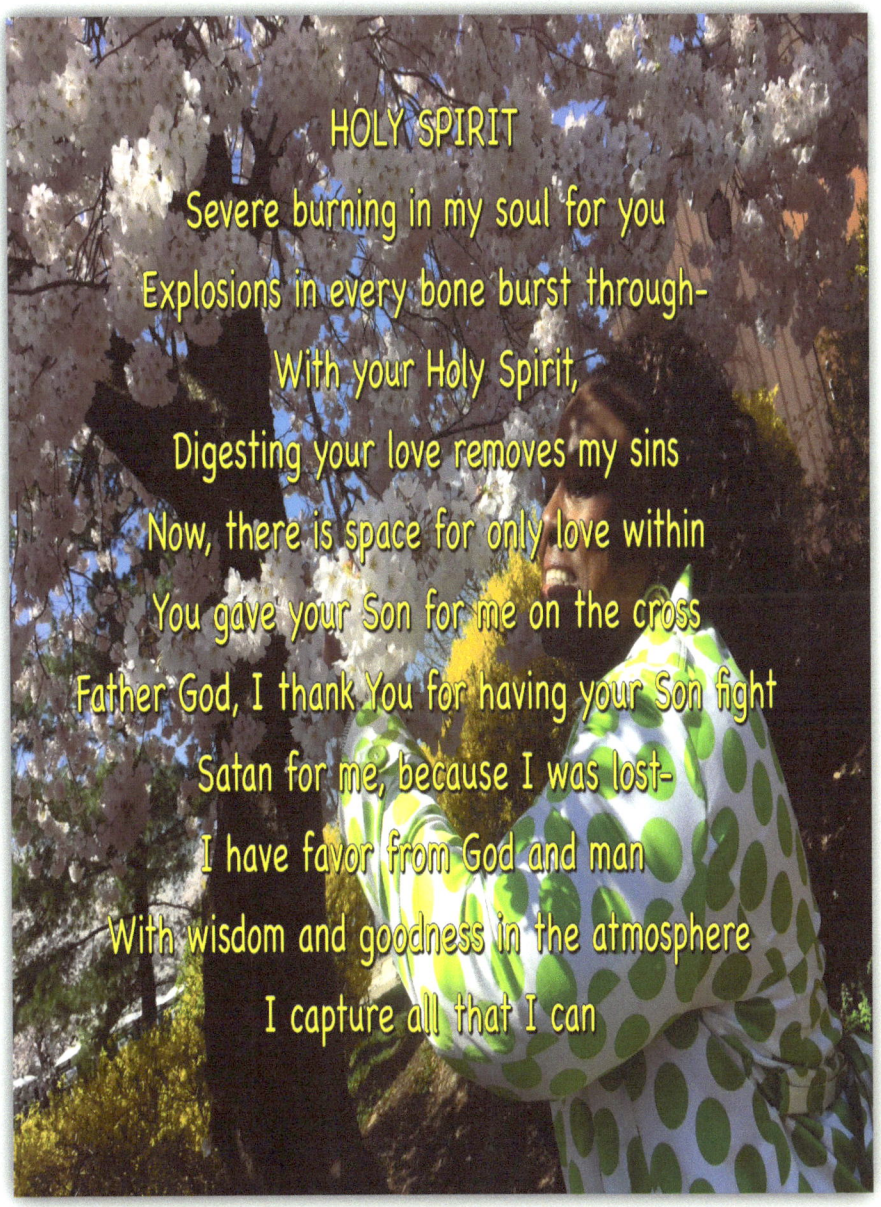

HOLY SPIRIT

Severe burning in my soul for you

Explosions in every bone burst through-

With your Holy Spirit,

Digesting your love removes my sins

Now, there is space for only love within

You gave your Son for me on the cross

Father God, I thank You for having your Son fight

Satan for me, because I was lost-

I have favor from God and man

With wisdom and goodness in the atmosphere

I capture all that I can

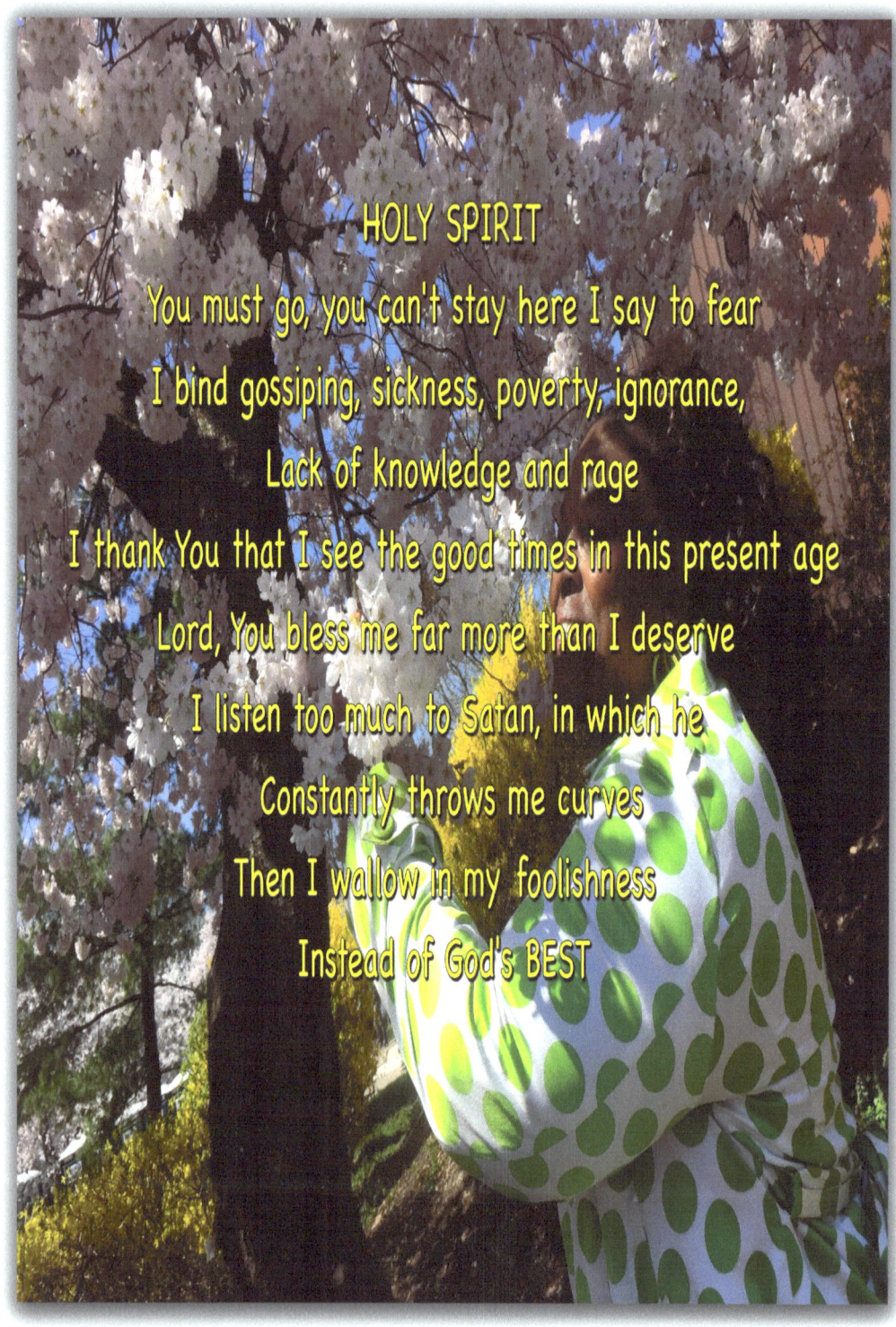

Gratitude

Thank You, Lord, *for pouring your spirit on my offspring and Your blessings on my children.*
Thank You, Lord, *that my children are sprouting up like a tree in the grass, like poplars (beauty) beside channels of water.* (Isaiah 44:3-4 NET)
Thank You for wisdom and knowledge.
Thank You, Lord, *that my children and family members are humbling themselves before you. For only you can exalt them.* (James 4:10 AMP)

Footsteps

Whatever you would have multiplied to you; do it.
If love is what you desire, show someone love. You are saved by grace. Show goodness and kindness today.
You are not under the law. Be quiet and listen for God's directions.
You must have a sensitive ear for what God wants you to do daily.
Love does not kill, steal, or destroy.
Do not repeat gossip. Encourage someone today. It is impossible to be perfect under the law.
Strive to show love.
The battle is in the mind. Sin starts in the mind. You have control of your thoughts.
Sow positive seeds so that you can receive a positive harvest.
Faith defeats Satan. Without faith, you please Satan. With faith, you please God.

Prayer

Precious Father,
Increase my faith in You. Help me to stay focused on You so that I can keep my mind on all that is right, just, and fair. Help me show more love and

plant good seeds daily. I need to become wise in Your word. Fill me completely with Your powerful Holy Spirit. I am striving every day to have a productive life. Help me humble myself, be patient and kind. You said that Jesus died so that I could dominate sin, not let sin dominate me. I believe that I can walk more each day in love. Because Jesus was struck repeatedly on the cross so that I can live forever in His eternal love, I believe that I can demonstrate more faith and love during my difficult situations.

Promises and Power

For sin shall not have dominion over you: for ye are not under the law, but under grace. (Romans 6:14).

Those who live as their human nature tells them to have their minds controlled by what human nature wants. Those who live as the Spirit tells them to have their minds controlled by what the Spirit wants. To be controlled by human nature results in death; to be controlled by the Spirit results in life and peace. And so, people become enemies of God when they are controlled by their human nature, for they do not obey God's law, and in fact they cannot obey it. Those who obey their human nature cannot please God. But you do not live as your human nature tells you to; instead, you live as the Spirit tells you to—if, in fact, God's Spirit lives in you. Whoever does not have the Spirit of Christ does not belong to him. But if Christ lives in you, the Spirit is life for you because you have been put right with God, even though your bodies are going to die because of sin. If the Spirit of God, who raised Jesus from death, lives in you, then he who raised Christ from death will also give life to your mortal bodies by the presence of his Spirit in you.

So then, my friends, we have an obligation, but it is not to live as our human nature wants us to. For if you live according to your human nature, you are going to die; but if by the Spirit you put to death your sinful actions, you will live. Those who are led by God's Spirit are God's children. For the Spirit that God has given you does not make you slaves and cause you to be afraid; instead, the Spirit makes you God's children, and by the Spirit's power we cry out to God, "Father! My Father!" God's Spirit joins himself to our spirits to declare that we are God's children. Since we are his children, we will possess the blessings he keeps for his people, and we will also possess with Christ what God has kept for him; for if we share Christ's suffering, we will also share his glory (Romans 8:5-17 GNT).

Everything God created is good. Nothing should be rejected if it is received with prayers of thanks (1 Timothy 4:4 GWT).

I delight in following your commands more than in having great wealth (Psalms 119:14 GNT).

Do you see what this means—all these pioneers who blazed the way, all these veterans cheering us on? It means we'd better get on with it. Strip it down, start running—and never quit! No extra spiritual parasitic sins. Keep your eyes on Jesus, who both began and finished this race we're in. Study how He did it. Because He never lost sight of where He was headed—that exhilarating finish in and with God—he could put up with anything along the way: Cross, shame, whatever. And now he's there, in the place of honor, right alongside God. When you are flagging in your faith, go over that story again item by item, that long litany of hostility he plowed through. That will shoot adrenaline into your souls (Hebrews 12:1-3 MSG).

I Have Spoken!

I will not be judgmental.
I will plant a seed of love today.
I will love God with all my heart and soul.
I will be more excited about following God's plan than increasing wealth.
I will see the kindness and goodness in others.
Today I will allow the Lord to use me.
I praise God for allowing me to have great compassion for others.

My Faults are in a Vault

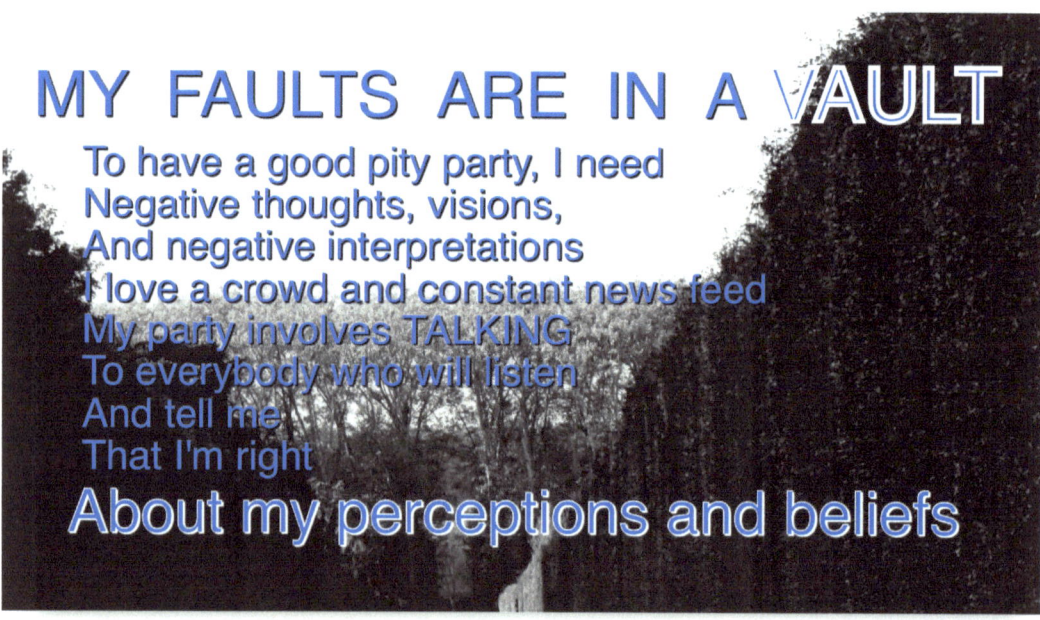

MY FAULTS ARE IN A VAULT

To have a good pity party, I need
Negative thoughts, visions,
And negative interpretations
I love a crowd and constant news feed
My party involves TALKING
To everybody who will listen
And tell me
That I'm right
About my perceptions and beliefs

I Know Why Birds Fight For A Position On The Power-Line

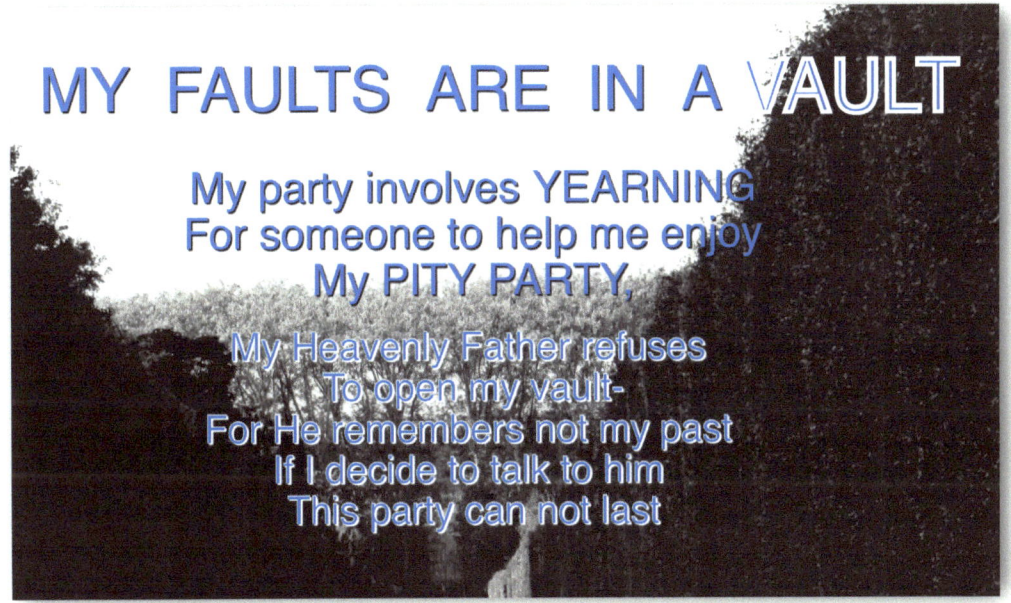

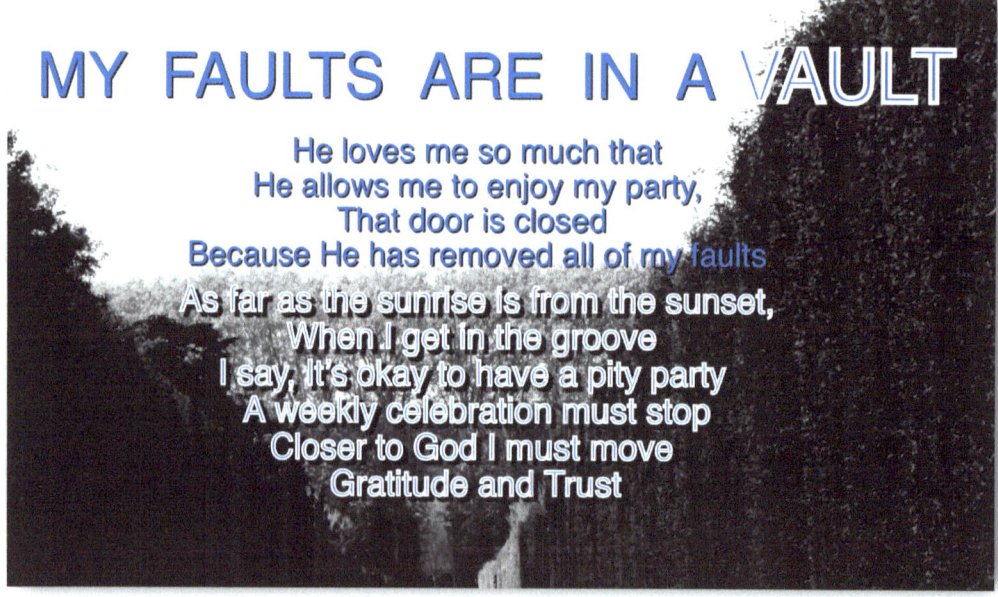

MY FAULTS ARE IN A VAULT

He loves me so much that
He allows me to enjoy my party,
That door is closed
Because He has removed all of my faults

As far as the sunrise is from the sunset,
When I get in the groove
I say, It's okay to have a pity party
A weekly celebration must stop
Closer to God I must move
Gratitude and Trust

Gratitude

Father, thank You for directing my path every day.
Father, thank You for teaching me how to forgive and forget so I can move forward.
Father, thank You for loving me enough to have Your Son to die for all of my mishaps.

Footsteps

Forgive.
Pray that you will be able to forget hurts and pain.
When you learn how to forgive and forget you will see miracles. You will experience peace as you never have before.
Life will not be a huge struggle.
Take control of your thoughts by changing them to good thoughts. Love will flow easier.
Healing will come quicker.
You can do all things through Christ who gives strength.
Christ will give you the strength to forgive and forget.

Prayer

Precious Father,
I know that You spoke everything into existence because only You are that powerful. Lord, I thank You for giving me peace beyond all understanding.
I thank You for loving me unconditionally and beyond all measures.
Help me engage only in mature, godly, holy, and wise behaviors.
I pray that resentment, hatred, and unforgiveness will cease in each one of my family members and others all over the world.
I will not worship other gods. I will worship only the God who spoke everything into existence. I cast down pride and seek humility. l cast down

ungratefulness, and daily demonstrate a grateful and thankful spirit. In the name of Jesus, I cast down sickness, mental illness, anger, negative thoughts, bitterness, maliciousness, gossiping, cruelty, lack of forgiveness, all diseases and addictions. I seek wholeness, wellness, love, oneness, a sound mind, wisdom, knowledge, understanding and the word of God as I would seek silver and gold. I will not be guided by "fear, insanity, confusion, illicit sex, perversion, promiscuity, idolatry, drug use, alcoholism, division, hatred, unlawfulness, (rivalry) jealousy, angry outbursts, selfish ambition, conflict, factions, envy, drunkenness, wild partying, and things like that."
I will be guided by the word of God, the love of God, Jesus Christ, God-sent angels, the power of God, and the Holy Spirit.

But if the Spirit is leading you, you are not under the law. The wrong things the sinful self does are clear: being sexually unfaithful, not being pure, taking part in sexual sins, worshiping gods, doing witchcraft, hating, making trouble, being jealous, being angry, being selfish, making people angry with each other, causing divisions among people, feeling envy, being drunk, having wild and wasteful parties, and doing other things like these. I warn you now as I warned you before: Those who do these things will not inherit God's kingdom (Galatians 5:19-21 NCV).

Promises and Power

I will forgive them for the wicked things they did, and I will not remember their sins anymore (Hebrews 8:12 NCV).

The Holy Spirit also tells us about this. First, he says: "This is the agreement I will make with them at that time, says the Lord. I will put my teachings in their hearts and write them on their minds. Then he says: "Their sins and the evil things they do— I will not remember anymore" (Hebrew 10:16,17 NCV).

God can erase all memory of your sin from His mind. If God can erase everyone's sins from His mind, for He can surely erase all of your sins from your mind. God is sovereign. God knows all and is everywhere at the same time. He has the power to see all and not allow sin and disobedience to live in His mind. God is omnipotent. How amazing it is that God forgives you for your sins, gives grace and mercy, and then He forgets about all sin. You must try harder to be as the Father. You need to forgive yourself and others (friends and enemies).

The only time you should look back over your life is to thank God for all He has done for you and ask Him to show you what actions you need to put in place to continue to move in a positive direction.

I Have Spoken!

I will practice love, kindness and goodness.
I will not look back. I will look ahead.
I refuse to focus on regrets and resentments.
I will forgive and forget. I expect to witness miracles.
I will forgive my friends, enemies, and loved ones.
I will not actively engage in sinful and evil behavior.
I praise God for permanently deleting all my sins and allowing fresh memories to exist.

A Prayer for a Teenager

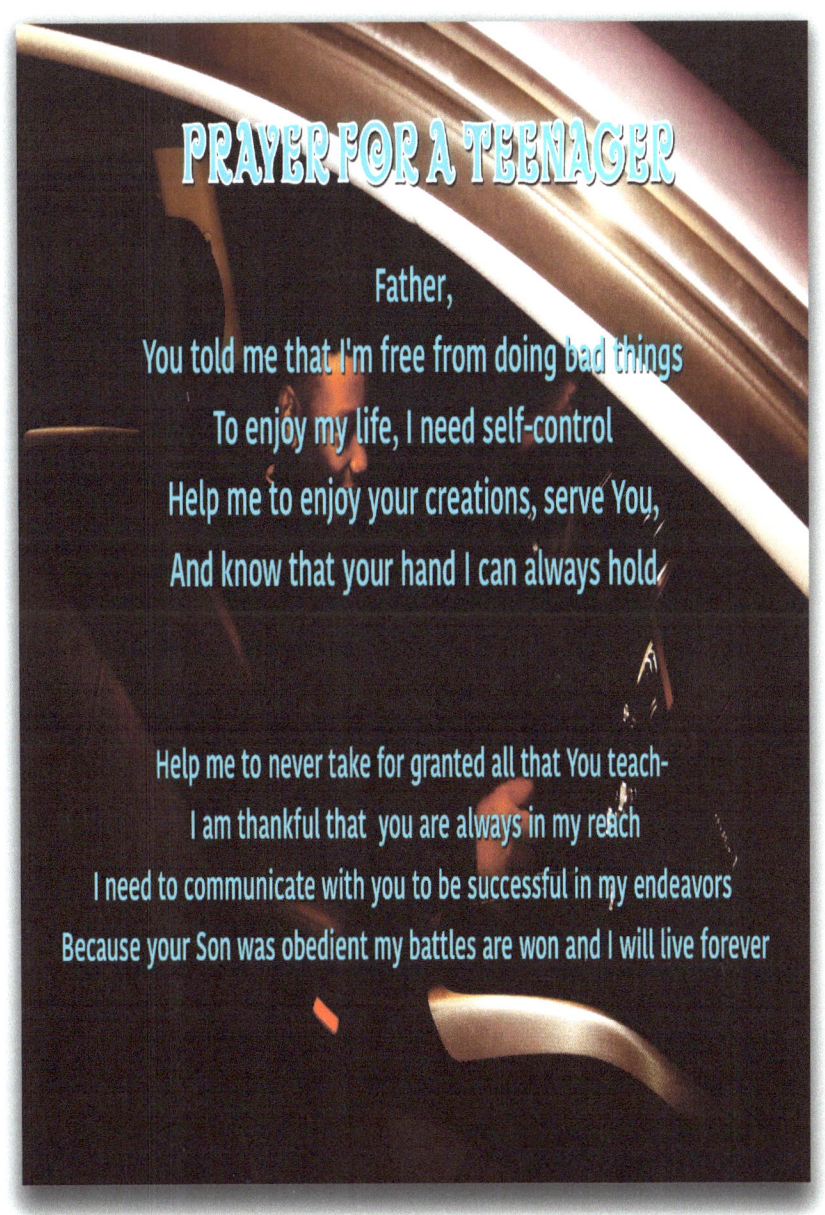

PRAYER FOR A TEENAGER

The hardest years are when you are in your teens

I know that You know more about me

Than I will ever know about myself

I really want to get to know you better

At my age, everything in my life matters

I need my Lord wherever I go

I need more knowledge and wisdom

Everyday in my life to consistently soar

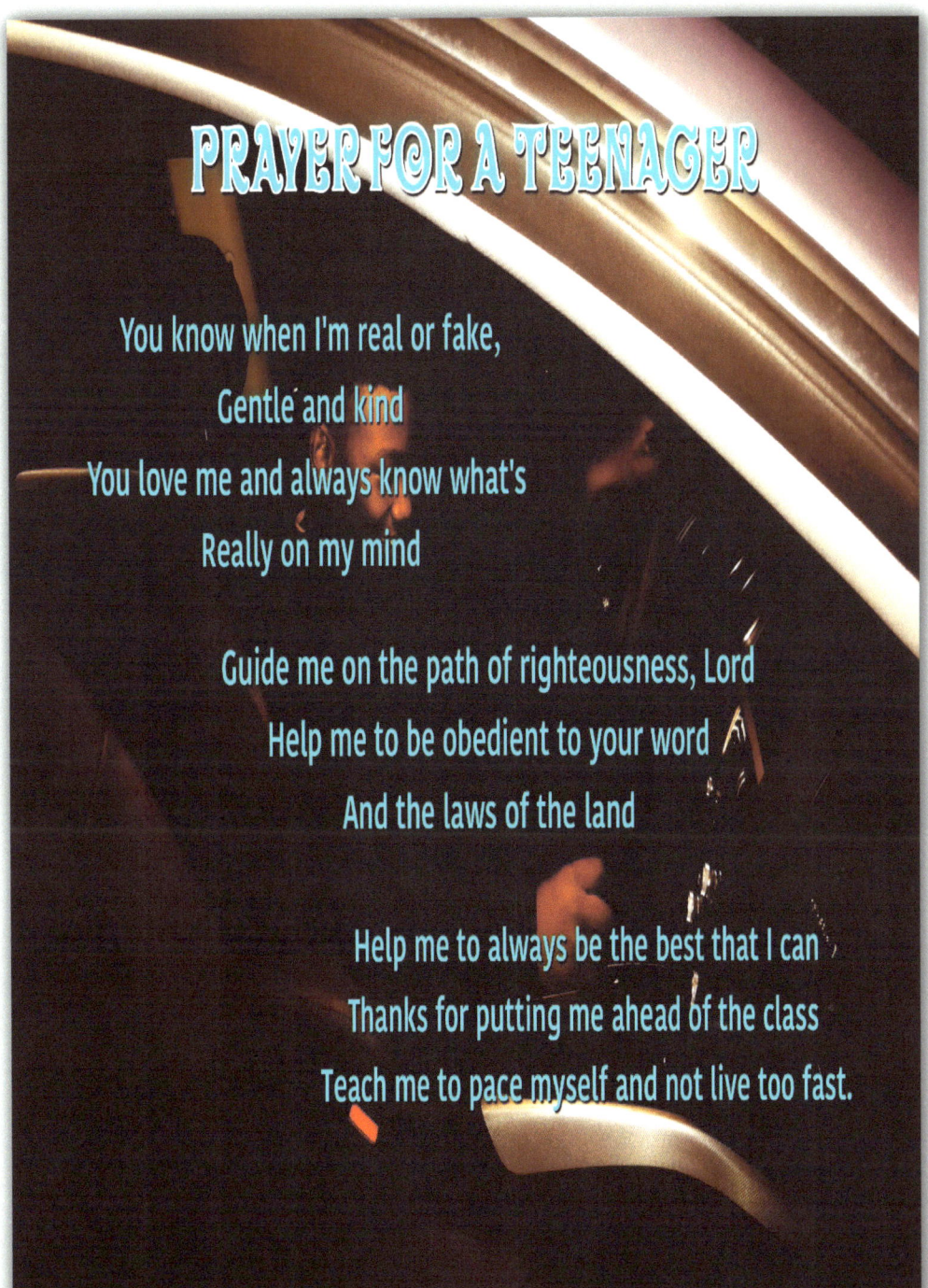

PRAYER FOR A TEENAGER

You know when I'm real or fake,
Gentle and kind
You love me and always know what's
Really on my mind

Guide me on the path of righteousness, Lord
Help me to be obedient to your word
And the laws of the land

Help me to always be the best that I can
Thanks for putting me ahead of the class
Teach me to pace myself and not live too fast.

PRAYER FOR A TEENAGER

Help each of us to pick up one another when we fall

In the mind of God, no one is too small

Help me to walk through life with a purpose of

Expressing gratitude for your sacrificial gift, that I don't deserve

Your love encourages me to have faith

Whether my path is straight or with many curves

I know that only You can keep me safe through all life mazes

I need to keep my eyes on You and never forget that,

You are King

Which gives me strength to encourage others when I am stumbling

PRAYER FOR A TEENAGER

Friends I will love as well as my haters

Help me to be a giver and never a taker

Above all, teach me to be careful of what I say

Help me to practice honesty and

Never desire the skills of a liar

For these are some virtues

That I will like to acquire

Help me walk through life knowing that You are near me always

Then I will understand that I must love all and not become a hater

For this is necessary to live life to the fullest

Instead of living life upon a hit and a miss, and

Never understanding complete rest

For only your protection will keep me safe,

Which demonstrates my desire to give you praise

Gratitude

Father, thank You for loving me and not giving me what I deserve.
I appreciate your compassion and kindness.
I thank You for doing more than I asked.
Thank You for placing the right people in my life at the right time.

Footsteps

Don't waste your breath on fools, for they will despise the wisest advice (Proverbs 23:9 NLT).

Strive to make wise decisions daily.
Put your focus on doing what's right and fair; then the money will come.
Act on good advice, don't just listen.
Use your own head.
Don't allow others to think for you. Analyze.

Prayer

Precious Father,
Help me to appreciate and love my parents.
Help me humble myself and refrain from being rude and boastful.
Help me show compassion toward others when they are hurting.
Help me speak the best of others and not engage in spreading gossip.
Help me be quick to forgive others and not keep a record of their wrongdoings.
Help me withdraw from confrontational and angry situations.
Help me allow others to go ahead and know that I don't always have to be first. Help me be honest and faithful.
Help me to always move forward, persevere and have great expectations.
Help me grace my brain with good thoughts.

Promises and Power

Listen to me, my child. Take seriously what I am telling you, and you will live a long life. I have taught you wisdom and the right way to live. Nothing will stand in your way if you walk wisely, and you will not stumble when you run. Always remember what you have learned. Your education is your life — guard it well. Do not go where evil people go. Do not follow the example of the wicked (Proverbs 4:10-14 GNB). *If you belong to Christ, then you are the descendants of Abraham and will receive what God has promised* (Galatians 3:29 GNT).

Turn at my rebuke; surely, I will pour out my spirit on you; I will make my words known to you. But whoever listens to me will dwell safely, and will be secure, without fear of evil (Proverbs 1:23, 33 NKJV).

If only you had listened when I corrected you, I would have told you what's in my heart; I would have told you what I am thinking. But those who listen to me will live in safety and be at peace, without fear of injury (Proverbs 1:23, 33 NCV).

I Have Spoken!

These hands will create and not con or take advantage of others.
These hands will heal and not destroy.
These hands will give and not take.
These hands will mend and not rip apart.
These hands will protect and not rob.
These hands will comfort and encourage and not discourage.
These hands will sow good seeds and not bully.
These hands will love and not hate.
These hands surrender all to the Jehovah God so that I can become productive and may become a mentor to others.
Father God, I surrender my tongue to be used for Your glory.

In my tongue is life and not death. I strengthen my relationship by speaking the Word in the face of any circumstance.
I will never degrade or intimidate, but always uplift.
I praise God for shining His bright light into my spirit.

The Lion's Den

THE LION'S DEN

Thank You Lord, for not giving me what I deserve

You hear and answer all the prayers,

You watch over me

As I am too blind to see

That the path I was on did not lead me to victory,

For You kept me from the lion's den

Which was running down the road of sin

I thought that I was the intelligent one,

Your sight is far greater than my imagination

Not knowing that only God gives wisdom,

For my thoughts will never be your thoughts,

The path that I take without You,

Will never be the right way

My path will be dark and take a lifetime

Your path will take less than a day and have lots of

Sunshine

Gratitude

Father,
I am thankful that You are my Father.
I will always have all I need because You are true to Your promises.
You allow me rest and relax comfortably.
You lead me to beautiful waterfalls where I am completely refreshed and mesmerized.
You light up the path that I am led down.
I am not afraid, even when there is no light, I don't know where I'm going, and feel alone.
I know that I am always safe and under Your wings.
I am honored because You allow others to see Your love for me.
You constantly give more and more to my family and me.
Your kindness and love are eternal.

Footsteps

Meditate on These
I live by faith of the Son of God, who loved me and gave Himself for me.

1. I am saved by grace and not my good works.
2. I am not holy because of what I do, but because God has made me holy.
3. I know that without God I am spiritually dead.
4. *I know that without God I can do nothing; however, I can do all things through Christ who gives me strength.* (Philippians 4:13 KJV)
5. God has control over the air.
6. God is rich in mercy and grace.
7. God loved me from the very beginning. God gave me all that I needed from the beginning of time.
8. God loves me unconditionally. His love for me is unchanged, unchanging, and unchangeable.
9. God's love is forever, which is through eternity.

Prayer

Precious Father,
I have always put my trust and strength in what I thought I should do for myself.
I realize that it is the Father who gives the increase, for only you have power to move my family and my life forward.
I thought that I had the power to do all those good things.
My love was not unconditional; my love was based on emotions. I didn't know that eternal love existed.
I thank You, Lord, that You have taught me how to deal with my emotions. My love for You can change because of my emotions. You loved us before the foundation of the world. You will love us in the world to come.

Promises and Power

For I know the thoughts that I think toward you, said the LORD, thoughts of peace, and not of evil, to give you an expected end. (Jeremiah 29:11-13 KJV)

For You (God the Father) know the plans You have for me and my family declares the Lord, plans to prosper me and my family and not harm us, plans to give us hope and a future.

Because I have called upon You and prayed to You, and The Father listened to me. I sought You and found You — yes, I sought You with all my heart.
His Spirit in your inner being gives you strength.
Give thanks to the Lord, for He is good; His love endures forever. Let them give thanks to the Lord for His unfailing love; and His wonderful deeds for mankind.
Let the one who is wise heed these things and ponder the loving deeds of the Lord (Psalm 107:1, 21, 43 NIV).

I Have Spoken!

I declare Father God,
That I will be a doer of Your word and not a hearer only.
I will seek ye first the kingdom of God and His righteousness and all things will be added unto me.
I will not allow my emotions to hinder my daily communication with God.
I will be *sober, and (constant) vigilant; because Satan walks about like a roaring lion, seeking whom he may devour.* (1 Peter 5:8 NKJV).
I praise God for blessing me, particularly at times, when He's not included in my ways and thoughts.

Old Fashioned Common Sense

Don't give me money without compassion

Don't give me money without your guidance

Don't give me money without a purpose

Please cleanse me, give me wisdom, knowledge, wealth and

Most importantly

C-O-M-M-O-N SENSE

Lord, help me to show what I can not feel,

Help my expressions and actions be real

Give me knowledge that only You have –

Teach me to give so that others will laugh

Help me to dream when I don't know

What –

For I know that your blessings and gifts could never be Just luck

Grant me a relationship with you that is not casual but extreme –
Not passive but intense
When I remain in your love, I know that I will marvel in
Good Old Fashioned Common Sense

Good health and strength are wealth

Happiness is wealth

Wisdom is wealth

Knowledge is wealth

Understanding is wealth

Sound judgment and good sense will watch over me
Wisdom will protect me from liars and evil schemes

Gratitude

Father, thank You for guarding my path.
Father, thank You for giving me wisdom and guarding my mind and heart.
Father, thank You for helping me understand what is just, right, and fair.
Father, thank You for knowledge, understanding, and common sense.

Footsteps

Select wise friends, not fools.
Seek ways to gain knowledge and understanding about truth, compassion, and righteousness.
Do not make quick decisions. Do research. Ask questions.
Think. Read the Bible in various versions.

Prayer

Precious Father,
Please give me wisdom to get through my daily activities. Help me seek knowledge, wisdom, and understanding daily. Help me be honest and walk with integrity.
Increase my faithfulness in Your will and Your ways.
For I know that with wisdom, I will be saved from evil people.

Promises and Power

For whoever finds me [Wisdom] finds life and draws forth and obtains favor from the Lord (Proverbs 8:35 AMP).

If any of you lacks wisdom, he should ask God, who gives generously to all without finding fault, and it will be given to him (James 1:5 NIV).

For the LORD gives [skillful and godly] wisdom; From His mouth come knowledge and understanding. He stores away sound wisdom for the righteous [those who are in right standing with Him]; He is a shield to those who walk in integrity [those of honorable character and moral courage], (PROVERBS 2:4, 6-7 AMP).

I Have Spoken!

I will make wise decisions.
I will search for wisdom daily and allow it to enter my heart.
I will ask God for answers.
Come and listen to my counsel.
I'll share my heart with you and make you wise.
"But all who listen to me will live in peace, untroubled by fear of harm." (Proverbs 1:23, 33 NLT) "*Your word is a lamp to my feet and a light for my path.*" (Psalms 119:105, NIV).
I praise God for sharing His heart with me.

The Day I Cried for a Friend

THE DAY I CRIED FOR A FRIEND

You are not alone
There are angels and many humans all around
Silent He may be, but God is not gone
He knows your every need
He feels your pain
Regardless of the endless tears
You must endure

While believing that He understands
And knows all your fears
He sees all of the good that you have done
As He keeps you in the palm of His hand
He loves you so much
He gave His perfect son to die for you and me
You can't touch my child, He says to Satan,
THIS IS PRIVATE PROPERTY!!

Gratitude

Father, thank You for this beautiful day.
Thank You for clean hot water.
I am grateful to have supportive family and friends.

Footsteps

Begin to thank God for one thing such as one blooming flower, a beautiful sunrise, a good friend.
You will begin to see them multiply.
Show love to the Father. Speak to Him.
Tell Him that you love Him because He is omnipotent, omniscient, and omnipresence.
Tell God how powerful He has been in your life. (Repeat) Relax in His power, strength, and love.

Prayer

Precious Father,
I need to feel Your love right now, for these burdens are too hard for me to bear. Please continue to hold me in the palm of Your hand.
I know that without You I am spiritually dead. I know that without You I can do nothing; however, I can do all things through Christ who gives me strength. Your love for us is unchanged, unchanging, and unchangeable. It is eternal. You loved us before the foundations of the world. I will praise Your holy name. Your love is forever.

Promises and Power

"For I know the plans I have for you," declares the Lord, "plans to prosper you and not to harm you, plans to give you hope and a future. Then you will call on me and come and pray to me, and I will listen to you. You will seek me and find me when you seek me with all your heart (Jeremiah 29:11-13 NIV).

You were once dead because of your failures and sins. You followed the ways of this present world and its spiritual ruler. This ruler continues to work in people who refuse to obey God. All of us once lived among these people, and followed the desires of our corrupt nature. We did what our corrupt desires and thoughts wanted us to do. So, because of our nature, we deserved God's anger just like everyone else. But God is rich in mercy because of his great love for us. We were dead because of our failures, but he made us alive together with Christ. (It is God's kindness that saved you.) God has brought us back to life together with Christ Jesus and has given us a position in heaven with him. He did this through Christ Jesus out of his generosity to us in order to show his extremely rich kindness in the world to come. God saved you through faith as an act of kindness. You had nothing to do with it. Being saved is a gift from God. It's not the result of anything you've done, so no one can brag about it. God has made us what we are. He has created us in Christ Jesus to live lives filled with good works that he has prepared for us to do (Ephesian 2:1-10 GWT).

But his answer was: "My grace is all you need, for my power is greatest when you are weak." I am most happy, then, to be proud of my weaknesses, to feel the protection of Christ's power over me. I am content with weaknesses, insults, hardships, persecutions, and difficulties for Christ's sake. For when I am weak, then I am strong (2 Corinthians 12:9-10, GNBDC).

HIS SPIRIT IN OUR INNER BEING GIVES US STRENGTH.

Give thanks to the Lord, for He is good; His love endures forever. Let them give thanks to the Lord for His unfailing love and his wonderful deeds for mankind. Let the one who is wise heed these things and ponder the loving deeds of the Lord (Psalms 107:1, 21, 43 NIV).

God is our shelter and strength, always ready to help in times of trouble (Psalm 46:1 GNTD).

We'll call ourselves right if we are strong enough to get what we want. No one ever got anywhere by being weak (The Wisdom of Solomon 2:11 GNTD).
Hammer the points of your ploughs into swords and your pruning knives into spears. Even the weak must fight (Joel 3:10 GNBDC).

I Have Spoken!

I am strong.
I am strong!
I am strong!!
I am STRONG!!
I AM STRONG!!
I praise God for exalting and encouraging me.

Sometimes in this life you are too weak to pray for yourself.
God will give someone a deep conviction to pray for another person.
When you are sensitive to the Holy Spirit, you will know when to intercede for someone. Others will know when you need intercessory prayer. One of the most trying times in life is during the death of a loved one.

Get Up Now

Gratitude

Father God,
I praise You because You are good.
You have been good to me all the days of my life.
You were good to me when I didn't know how I would make it from one hour to the next.
I praise you, Lord, and give thanks unto the Lord, for Your mercy is forever.
Because You have delivered me from destructive behavior more times than I deserve, I glorify You.

Footsteps

Allow Jesus to pour His Spirit into you.
Live by love.
You will never be perfect under the law.
Strength comes when you give love to your neighbors. The victory is won!
Show love and have faith that God will meet your needs. Give God praise and show gratitude daily.
Strive for perfection in all things.
Console others rather than expect to be consoled or praised.

Prayer

Precious Father,
I thank You because I have been given victory through our Lord Jesus Christ. I had the victory all through my childhood when violence and diseases were all around. I had the victory when I was all alone as a child and only You could help me. I had the victory when I didn't know where my next meal was coming from. I had the victory when I was lost and couldn't find my way home, and You sent an angel to show me the way. I had the victory when You gave me the courage to say no to Satan's tactics when all my

friends said yes. I had the victory when I could walk away from bad relationships unharmed with what meant most to me.

I thank You, Lord, for ordering my steps when I didn't know I needed to have my steps ordered. I thank You, Lord, for guiding me in the right direction when I didn't know that I needed guidance. I thank You, Lord, for never leaving me or forsaking me when You could have allowed me to fall. Just as You kept Daniel out of the lion's den, You kept me from being eaten by wolves.

Unto thee, O my strength, will I sing: for God is my defense, and the God of my mercy (Psalms 59:17 KJV).

Promises and Power

They were hungry and thirsty and had given up all hope. Then in their trouble they called to the LORD, and He saved them from their distress. He led them by a straight road to a city where they could live. They must thank the LORD for his constant love, for the wonderful things He did for them. He satisfies those who are thirsty and fills the hungry with good things (Psalms 107:5-9 GNBDC).
He blessed them also, so that they are multiplied greatly; and suffered not their cattle to decrease (Psalms 107:6, 8, 22, 38 KJV). If He didn't allow the cattle to decrease, then He will not allow my children or other means to decrease.

I Have Spoken!

I can do nothing on my own.
I can do anything when I ask the Lord for help.
I will speak to the solution and not the problem.

(Example: If your child is not interested in being successful in school, say aloud, "My child will seek knowledge and wisdom as if it is gold. My child will be the head and not the tail.")

I praise God for giving me the authority to speak to my problems and believe they are solved.

Spirit of God

Spirit of God
Everything in me
Knows that I do not deserve
God's powerful Holy Spirit inside
He prepared to send his Son to Calvary
Before He created this body,
He love me so much that He gave
His spotless, sinless, only Son
The only perfect human being
To be killed for me; a hateful, filthy, sinner
He knew from the very beginning
That through His Son,
I would be a winner
He would rather watch
His Son die on the cross
To stop a torn, battered, and
Disgusted body from being loss
The Father decided to put
His Holy Spirit inside
This ugly filthy soul
If I allow
His Spirit inside of me, in Him I can hide
With added promises of protection
He will forever be my guide
There inside of me is the same Spirit
Inside my Jesus, inside my Jesus,

Kathy Buckner

There inside of me is the same Spirit
Inside my Jesus, inside my Jesus,
The One who was crucified
And was raised from the dead
For a person who was
Mean, ugly, evil and filthy,
Living without benefits
And full of pride
In this life I will never be worthy
Of His powerful Holy Spirit
That fills me inside
Satan did not die for anyone,
For he is getting free services
From many souls
Most contemplate about
Serving a righteous God
Satan does not make
The sun to rise
And rain to fall
So that there are
Beautiful flowers
And food to eat
From fruitful plants that
Grow big and tall
I boldly come to
Your throne

Gratitude

Thank You, Father, for placing Your Holy Spirit inside of me.
Thank You, Father, for allowing me to have happiness on earth.
Thank You, Father, for Your covenant blessings and promises.

Footsteps

Stop every morning to allow the Holy Spirit to lead you.
Gratitude and praises encourage the Holy Spirit.
Acknowledge the Holy Spirit as a person.
Keep your faith in the power of God.
But the anointing which ye have received of him abideth in you, and ye need not that any man teach you: but as the same anointing teacheth you of all things, and is truth, and is no lie, and even as it hath taught you, ye shall abide in him (1 John 2:27 KJV).

Prayer

Precious Father,
I bow down and worship You for having your Son to die on the cross for my salvation. I worship You for loving me unconditionally. I worship You because Your Son gave His life sacrificially for a dying world. I worship You with a sacrificial gift. I worship You for your majesty. I worship You in Spirit and Truth.
I worship You, Father God, because You keep my family under your wing and constantly cover us with the sacrificial blood of your son Jesus Christ, my Lord and Savior. I bow my head to worship You by obeying the word of God. I worship You, Jehovah God, because You redeemed my life from destruction over and over again and crowned me with loving kindness and tender mercies. I thank You for that, Father God. I bow down and praise and worship You for all these blessings.

For when God made promise to Abraham, because he could sware by no greater, (when You didn't have to) he sware by himself. (Hebrews 6:13 KJV)

Because I have made You, Lord, my refuge, and the Most High my dwelling place, there shall no evil befall me, nor any plague come near my tent. For You will give Your angels especial charge over me, to accompany and defend and preserve me in all my ways of obedience and service (Psalms 91:10 AMPC).

I worship You because You constantly watch each one of us. You created your angels to protect each of us day and night.

You gave Your Son so that wherever we are; we will have a Comforter.

Promises and Power

That your faith should not stand in the wisdom of men, but in the power of God. But we speak the wisdom of God in a mystery, even the hidden wisdom, which God ordained before the world unto our glory: But as it is written, eye hath not seen, nor ear heard, neither have entered into the heart of man, (the things which God hath prepared for them that love him.) Now we have received, not the spirit of the world, but the spirit which is of God; that we might know the things that are freely given to us of God. Which things also we speak, not in the words which man's wisdom teacheth, but which the Holy Ghost teacheth; comparing spiritual things with spiritual (1 Corinthians 2:5, 7, 9, 12, 13 KJV).

I assure you that it is better for you that I go away. If I don't go away, the Companion won't come to you. But if I go, I will send him to you. When he comes, he will show the world it was wrong about sin, righteousness, and judgment.

However, when the Spirit of Truth comes, he will guide you in all truth. He won't speak on his own, but will say whatever he hears and will proclaim to you what is to come. He will glorify me, because he will take what is mine and proclaim it to you. Everything that the Father has is mine. That's why I said that the Spirit takes what is mine and will proclaim it to you.

In that day, you won't ask me anything. I assure you that the Father will give you whatever you ask in my name. Up to now, you have asked nothing in my name. Ask and you will receive so that your joy will be complete (John 16:7-8, 13-15, 23-24 CEB).

I Have Spoken!

I believe in the Holy Spirit as I believe in God.
I will ask the Father for help when I am anxious or worrying about situation.
God has prepared for me more than I can see, hear, or imagine in my heart.
I will allow the Holy Spirit to teach me, along with His anointed ones.
I worship the Father in Spirit and Truth.
I praise God for the ultimate sacrifice of His son so that I may have a Comforter.

You are not Alone

Gratitude

Father God,
Thank You for the angels that you assigned to protect, defend, and preserve me.
Thank You for being my Father.
Thank You for showing me how to rest in You.
Father, I thank You for what You have done in the past, what You are doing now, and what You have done for the future.

Footsteps

Concentrate on taking one step at a time.
Have faith in God by focusing on what His word says.
Do not allow your feelings to overtake you.
Know that you are deeply loved and highly favored.

Promises and Power

Teach me to do your will, for you are my God; your Spirit is good. Lead me onto level ground (Psalms 143:10 LEB).
Give us help against the enemy because human assistance is worthless. With God we will display great strength. He will trample on our enemies (Psalms 108:12-13 GW).
You have rescued me from death. You have kept my feet from stumbling so that I could walk in Your presence, in the light of life (Psalms 56:13 GW).

Prayer

Precious Father,

Today I will float in God's love and be vigorous and strong.
I believe that God's word will take me higher than I can imagine or think.

I will take up permanent residence in a life of love and allow God to live in me. There is a purpose in life for everything that I do.

Trust is mandatory for success!
I will trust in God to use me for His purpose.

Let your gentleness be known to all men. The Lord is at hand. (Philippians 4:5 WEB) A person who's living from within always goes beyond.

Thank You for the Spirit of power, love, and a sharp mind that you allowed me to use.

Because you have made the LORD, [who is] my refuge, Even the Highest, your dwelling place, no evil will befall you, nor will any plague come near your tent. For He will command His angels to protect and defend and guard you in all your ways, [of obedience and service] (PSALM 91:9-11).

I Have Spoken!

The Lord is my helper, I will not fear. What can people do to me (Hebrews 13:6MEV)?
I will call those things that I don't see as if they are in front of my face. (John 14:12).
I praise God that I don't have to worry, for He fights all of my battles.

The Day I Threw a Kiss to the World

The day that I threw a kiss to the world
Burdens were lifted
Battlefield was quieter
Joy and love were prevailing
Perception grew richer
Steps were smoother
My purpose was brighter
On the waves of life,
I was sailing-
With a spirit filled body
Faults and complaints were few
My body lined up with an attitude
That was totally new
And a deepened vision of faithfulness
Grace was potent
Problem begin to lessen
I received the sweet favor that the Lord sent
Abundantly living
Smile grew bigger and laughter was louder
The day that I threw a kiss to the world
I felt it in my feet
My heart created a song
As I started dancing to the Creator's beat

Gratitude

Father, I thank You for a more pleasant attitude.
Father, I thank You for not giving up on me.
Father, I thank You for softening my perception and my heart so that I can enjoy life.
Father, I thank You for renewing my mind.
Father, I thank You for directing me along a path that enabled me to grow and feel the flow of your love.

Footsteps

Keep an open mind and heart.
Surrender all to God.
Allow God to use you on a path where you may not feel comfortable.
Walk in the plan of God daily.

Prayer

Precious Father,
You are the Father of our Savior Jesus Christ. Thank You, Lord for adopting me into Your family. You have made all preparations for me. You thought of me before You created the world. Help me walk in my purpose for being on this earth. Help me see all the good that's all around me. I will seek You first with all my heart and soul. I will walk in Your love, strength, and grace daily as I tell others of Your glory. I will live in my inheritance through Jesus Christ and intelligently engage in my purpose as I learn to discern Him personally.

Promises and Power

Blessed and worthy of praise be the God and Father of our Lord Jesus Christ, who has blessed us with every spiritual blessing in the heavenly realms in Christ, just as [in His love] He chose us in Christ [actually selected us for Himself as His own] before the foundation of the world, so that we would be holy [that is, consecrated, set apart for Him, purpose-driven] and blameless in His sight. The Spirit is the guarantee [the first installment, the pledges, a foretaste] of our inheritance until the redemption of God's own [purchased] possession [His believers], to the praise of His glory and [I pray] that the eyes of your heart [the very center and core of your being] may be enlightened [flooded with light by the Holy Spirit], so that you will know and cherish the hope [the divine guarantee, the confident expectation] to which He has called you, the riches of His glorious inheritance in the saints (God's people), (Ephesian 1:3-4, 14, 18, AMP).

I Have Spoken!

God tells us in His word "I want you to be wise about what is good, and innocent about what is evil (Romans 16:19, NIV)."

I will become knowledgeable about the things of God.

I receive the spirit of discernment and use it wisely.

I will increase my relationship with God so that I can see exactly what it is He is calling me to do.

I praise God because He tells me His secrets.

www.ingramcontent.com/pod-product-compliance
Lightning Source LLC
Chambersburg PA
CBHW042034150426
43201CB00002B/19